Published by:

Business Services Support Limited
PO Box 48097
London SE2 0WR
Email: Enquiries@businessservicessupport.com
Web: www.businessservicessupport.com

This edition published 2006 ©Sheila Elliott

ISBN 1-905803-10-9
ISBN 978-1-905803-10-1

British Library Cataloguing in publication data- A catalogue record for this book is available from the British Library

Printed in England

CONTENTS

This booklet is to be used only by the person to whom it is given. The material contained herein is the intellectual property of Business Services Support Limited. It is not to be stored, copied or reproduced either mechanically or electronically and we request that it is not to be communicated in whole or in part, to any third party without the express permission in writing of Business Services Support Limited.

Introduction

In every business, people need to communicate and interact with each other in a bid to undertake their key responsibilities successfully. The nature of interactions that take place between people may differ considerably depending on their roles within the organisation. Moreover, it is through social interactions that people get to influence others, sometimes successfully, at other times not so successfully.

"Influencing" is very much at the heart of every business. Without successful influencing, organisations will be unable to make good progress towards the accomplishment of their corporate goals and objectives.

In this manual, we will provide you with:
- Details of what influencing skills are, as well as their importance in business intercourse.
- An in depth information of what makes a successful influencer and why people resist being influenced.
- Strategies and guidance on how to develop your influencing skills.

The purpose of this manual is to help you gain an understanding of the skills you must have and develop to build your capacity to influence others successfully. We say successfully, because it is possible to influence people without getting any genuine commitments from them- something akin to having people with you, whilst their minds and souls are elsewhere.

In summary, this manual provides details of:

3

- What influencing skills are.
- The importance of influencing skills.
- The key qualities of people who are consistently successful in influencing others.
- The different influencing styles.
- Indicators of a trained listener and an untrained listener.
- The importance of communicating effectively.
- The attributes of assertive behaviours
- How to question others effectively in different situations.

Chapter 1

What is influencing

Influencing is the art of getting others to do what we want them to do. Sometimes, it can be achieved through genuine commitment and belief in the influencer's suggestions, proposals or behaviours. Other times it can be achieved by the use of aggressive medium, threats or one's formal power or authority. Whatever the means used to influence others, influencing is concerned with getting one's way.

In practice, there are various ways people can be influenced by others. Most of these media will be covered extensively in this manual later. However, it is best to establish at this point that not all forms of influencing skills are good. Using the right type of influencing strategy can protect long-term relationships, whilst at the same time getting the other party to change their actions or behaviours. Similarly, when influencing is carried out using the wrong medium, long-term relationships can be put at risk and the gains achieved through influencing the other person can be short lived.

Influencing is a very important part of human relationships. Whether in a formal or an informal setting, humans are constantly relating to one another and on many occasions, getting others to buy into their belief (or not, as the case may be). In an organisational setting, managers and leaders alike need to be able to positively influence their staff to achieve corporate goals. A business must also be able to influence customers to purchase their services or products consistently, if it is to succeed in its market.

5

Who do we influence?

Throughout our lives, we are consistently influencing one another, sometimes in good ways, at other times in less than favourable ways. Let us look at this point in some detail.

As individuals- We influence our friends, spouses and partners to buy particular types of products/services (purchase of holiday deals, washing machines, televisions, cars etc) or to buy from particular suppliers.
We influence our relatives in their purchasing decisions, as well as in decisions relating to problems and challenges of life. We give them advice on what they should do or not do.

As parents or guardian- We influence our dependants on how they should behave, dress, eat and so forth.

As a staff member- We influence our colleagues on how they should approach their work, how they should conduct themselves to achieve good results, how they should tackle specific challenges, what to say and not to say in public areas etc.

As a manager- We influence the actions of staff that we manage. We influence the way they behave at work, the way they relate with others and their attitude to work and so forth.

As a leader- We influence the direction of organisations - e.g. where resources should be invested, what changes should be made and when, what systems should be put in place and when, what types of resources are required and how they are to be allocated across the organisations.

6

As suppliers of services and products- We influence the purchasing behaviour of markets.

This can be achieved through actions taken to produce new products; promote new products; provide incentives to customers to get them to purchase our products instead of the competition.

As buyers of services and products – We influence suppliers to give us better quality of services in the form of speedy delivery of services or better terms and conditions of services.

As members of the community- We influence the community through our actions or inactions. We lobby political groups to make changes to legislations, we elect people we believe will best serve our interests in government and so forth.

So, as you can see from the above analysis, our sphere of influence is wide ranging, indeed.

Influencing another person to change their behaviour or accept another point of view is not without its challenges. People are different in many respects; they have diverse needs and are motivated differently. If we are to get people to do what we want them to do, we must understand them so that we can determine the best influencing strategy to employ. We must be able to know what makes them tick, what turns them off, how do they think, what is important to them and how is this manifested in the way they behave.

The dynamics of human behaviour

People have diverse needs, values, abilities, talents, personalities and preferences. They are motivated by different factors and have likes and dislikes. This diversity in characteristics implies that the approach to influencing people needs to be flexible.

7

This flexibility of approach will be more appreciated as we now look at some of these points in more detail.

When it comes to looking at personalities, people think differently and perceive things differently. As a result, it is not unusual for people to describe the same event differently or even interpret similar information differently. Sadly, most of the conflicts that exist between humans are precisely driven by these differences, which most people fail to acknowledge. Being different has tremendous benefits, but it can equally give rise to tremendous challenges.

Over the years, a number of tools have been devised to diagnose different personality traits. A common tool used by many management consultants is "The Myers Briggs Personality Test". This tool shows stunning differences between the way people think, perceive the world and make decisions. For instance, when some people are processing information, they have a strong preference to rely extensively on external evidence that is collected, analysed and evaluated. Others may rely on their intuition, which is less related to the external evidence available to them (something akin to their gut feeling). Others make use of a blend of the two preferences, knowing fully that each preference has it weaknesses and strengths.

Then there is the issue of how people make decisions. Some people rely predominately on logical thinking, whereas others rely on their feelings. The logical thinkers do not put too much reliance on people's emotions, as their primary goal is to be objective in their decision-making. Those who are feelers are predominately concerned about people's emotions when making decisions. And of course, there are those who tend to take the mid position.

8

There are also people who are extroverts and derive their energy from being with others. For them being sociable is important and anyone who is not like them could potentially be labelled as unsociable.

People in this category tend to have strong social network. They are known by many and can be a great source of soliciting invaluable information from their network. The opposite of the extroverts are the introverts, who have a different approach to life. Their energy source comes from within and they take pride in spending time on their own to reflect. People in this category tend to be imaginative and creative.

Then again there are people who are great planners. They like everything to be stable and orderly. They rarely cope well in unpredictable environments. They prefer meetings with formal agendas so that they know in advance what to expect. At the opposite pole to these people are those who prefer uncertainties and cope very well in unstable environments. In practice, every organisation needs these different personalities in the right balance to cope with different situations. For instance, a business that is lacking in introverts will find it difficult to come up with creative and imaginative ideas. Similarly, a business that has limited extroverts will find it difficult to form networks that are useful for information exchange. Furthermore, whereas logical thinkers can reach objective decisions without being prejudiced by their feelings for others, feelers can find it difficult to make decisions outside their emotions. However, with feelers, their feelings could bring some balance in situations requiring objectivity and sensitivity. For instance, in a change management situation requiring staff redundancy, management needs to make objective decisions but in implementing their decisions they must be sensitive to the feelings of staff.

If we take this discussion a step further, you will see that when it comes to learning, people's preferences are also different. Some people learn through observations followed by practical implementation of what have been learnt. Others learn through formal training followed by practical implementation of what have been learnt and so forth. People who are pragmatists (i.e. learn by doing), sometimes find it frustrating when they see others taking a different approach.

In terms of motivation, whereas some people are motivated by financial rewards, recognition, praise (mainly extrinsic values). Others are self-motivated. Their motivation comes from within.
For instance, they are motivated by being able to carry out challenging tasks (i.e. activities that stretch them).

Understanding and motivating

Despite the impact of our beliefs, experiences and cultures, in our assessment and evaluation of information, modern research on the brain suggests that we all have unique ways of thinking and processing information. We experience the world based on how we individually use our brains. Some of us think in linear sequences, others automatically envisage as larger whole, some people like lots of flexibility and wide ranging discussions, others prefer to know exactly what's what and others want clear rules and guidelines.

Therefore, when we interact with others, for instance at meetings, every participant has a slightly different experience of the session. Each person has a different perception and interpretation of what was discussed, different comfort zones and different expectations.

10

For you, this has some practical implications. You must be aware that people have different learning styles, different approaches to how and what they hear, and are motivated by different factors. To help you recognise the main differences between people, consider some of the following spectra drawn from NLP (Neuro Linguistic Programming).

Internal/ external

- About 40% of people are internally driven. They just know that what they think or feel to be right is right. They evaluate their own performance based on their own standards and criteria. They resist when someone tells them what to do or decides for them. Their body language is likely to be sitting upright, pointing to self, minimal gesture or facial expressions. The best way of communicating with internal people is to use phrases like, **"it's up to you" "only you can decide", "Have a go and see what you think".**

- About 40% of people are externally driven. They want to know what others think. They need external validation of their views. External information is often taken as an order or instruction. Their body language leans back and watches carefully for signals from those around them. The best way of communicating with external people is to use third party endorsement, and phrases such as "**it will go down well with others"; "you'll get a lot of brownie points".**

  External people are likely to need lots of feedback and encouragement to stay motivated.

11

- About 20% of people are in the middle of the spectrum (equally internal and external).

General/Specifics

- 60% of people are general people. They prefer to see the big picture and are bored by details. They are likely to present things in random order, talk in concepts and abstracts. To get through to them use words like **"essentially", "an overview", "generally".**
- 15% are specific people. They want details. Without them your words will seem to them, superficial and unconvincing. You can recognise specific people because they tend to use lots of adverbs and adjectives, speak in sequences (step by step, often returning to the beginning of the story if they lose their place). To influence/ motivate them you will need to use words like **"specifically", "exactly", "precisely" and "the key point".**

Proactive/reactive

- 15%-20% of people are proactive. They are the initiators and they can be impatient to get things done. They often act without due consideration. They want to put their stamp on what's going on. Their language is likely to contain lot of active verbs and have a crisp clear sentence structure. They can sometimes be like steamrollers. Their body language is likely to be active, even fidgety. They may show signs of impatience. You will need to use proactive phrases to motivate them e.g. **"go for it"; "let's get going"; "what are we waiting for"; "why not just run with it"** etc.

12

- 15%-20% of people are reactive- they prefer to react to the views and actions of others. They may spend a lot of time thinking and analysing and then not take any action. They often believe in chance and luck. Their language is likely to be tentative, long sentences, lots of qualifiers- **perhaps, possibly**, lots of conditionals- **would, might, may** etc.

  You can get through to them with phrases such as, **"Let's look at this from all angles"; "Consider this"; "You might want to   think about"; "The time is right"; "Hang on a minute".**

Sameness/difference

- 70% Sameness- These people don't like change. They want things to remain the same. They usually like the familiar. They tend to be chameleon-like. Almost all people who like sameness are prepared to accept very occasional change, as long as it is put to them well. Sameness people look for common threads, they like continuity. Influence them by using word such as, **"like before", "unchanging", "the same, only better"**
- 20% Difference- They thrive on change, the bigger the better. People who like difference want to mark themselves out from the crowd. They want new experiences. They tend to use words such as **"new", "different", "changed"** and so forth. They are best influenced by words such **as "unique"; "unrecognisable"; "change the script"** and so forth.

Options/procedures

- Options (flexible) - Options people feel confined by rigid rules. They want scope to express themselves.

13

They see flexibility as a virtue. They are motivated by opportunities and possibilities to do something in a different way. They often create new systems and procedures but have a great deal of difficulty following them. They see procedures people as rigid and restricted. This type of people can be motivated by words such **as "opportunity", "unlimited possibilities**", and "**a whole new way of looking at the world".**

- Procedures (rule governed) people feel safest when they know exactly where they are and what is expected of them. Procedure people feel there is a right way of doing things. They like to know the rules. They take satisfaction from following rules faithfully. They tend to think that options people are all over the place. For this category of people, in order to motivate them you must provide very clear guidance on the ground rules for any exercise, **"First... then... followed by"**. They will want a clear programme for the day and will want to stick to it.

Towards/away from

- 40% of people are "towards" people. They are enthusiasts. If you want to persuade them toward a person, you will need to build their hopes and dreams. They have aims and goals and are enthused by achieving them. They tend to be optimists and not very good at identifying potential problems. They talk about what they can gain, achieve, get or have. Their body language tends to be enthusiastic and inclusive. Motivate them with words like, **"benefits"; "this should help you to", "achieve"** and so forth.

- 40% of people are "away from" people. They are distrustful of hopes and dreams. Solving problems motivates them. They tend to be pessimistic.

14

They are energised by threats (i.e. sticks, rather than carrots). They will respond to negative stimuli (so they will drop everything to fix something that is going wrong). They will tend to fight against something (e.g. injustice) rather than for something (e.g. freedom). In extreme cases, they can seem jaded and cynical towards people. Influence and motivate them by using words like **"avoid"; "watch out for"; "solve" and so forth.**

Using language to motivate

Influencing is about getting others to do what we want them to do. The language we use can either influence others positively or negatively. We can now look at some words that can positively influence others in our formal and informal communication.

Warm words
Warm words draw people towards you. Try to use warm words in your communication such as:
- Hope
- Trust
- Bold
- Commitment
- Sure
- Safe

Different senses
To influence others, we must be sensitive to the predominant senses a person uses to make decisions. Research suggests that we all have a dominant sense and this is the sense on which we rely most to interpret the world.

For example, for some people, their sight is the most important sense. They are very aware of their surroundings, the colour of a room, light and shade.

Those for whom hearing is the dominant sense will be very sensitive to sound (they are very aware of music playing in the background, of a radio that is not tuned in properly).

Other people are kinaesthetic (i.e. they like to touch and feel things) so the texture of clothes is important to them. They may be particularly sensitive to heat and cold.

When handling meetings, you can use these senses to help people understand the message. If you express your message in language that appeals to the senses, it will be more easily absorbed.

For instance:

- Can you see what I mean? I hope this is clear.
- Can you hear what I am saying? Does it sound right to you?
- Does this feel right to you? Can you pick up what I am saying?

Words that get through to visual people

- Light
- Bright
- Show
- See
- View

(e.g. **let's <u>show</u>** them we mean business)

16

Words that get through to aural people
- Attune
- Loud
- Hush
- Sound
- Listen

Example we have got to get our message across **loud** and clear.
Words that get through to kinaesthetic people

- Feel
- Tough
- Handle
- Soft
- Chaffing

(e.g. we must **pull** these people into the 21st century)

So why do we need to know all these aspects about people. Our capacity to influence others will depend on how well we know them and our ability to use that knowledge to our advantage.

To recap, you will see from the previous section that there are specific words that can be used to influence certain personalities. You will see that visual people are more likely to be influenced by visual descriptive words and so forth. Therefore, we believe that armed with this knowledge, you are already one step ahead of influencing others effectively.

Chapter 2

How do we influence

Influencing others, involves getting them to do what we want them to do. More often than not, our ability to influence others can arise from numerous sources. These sources vary considerably in their nature and to a large extent their effectiveness, as we shall soon see. Our ability to influence others comes from four key sources:
- Personality
- Expertise
- Information and network
- Position or status

Personality

People who are consistently successful in influencing others tend to behave in a particular way. They are usually charismatic and others identify with them easily. They generally have most or all of the following qualities:

- **Trustworthy**- Generally, people will only follow others when they believe in them. Otherwise they will resist any attempt to be influenced. Trust is an essential element in any relationship. When people believe in someone, they are willing to give them a chance and will accept their proposal unreservedly. However, trust is not something that is gained easily. It usually takes time and it involves the influencer demonstrating integrity and honesty over a reasonable period of time. When a person consistently behaves honestly and does what he/she promises to do, trust is gained over time.

18

Equally, trust is lost when a person consistently fails to live up to what they say they will do.

- **Confident**- People who believe in themselves are more likely to be taken seriously by others. Generally, the value one puts on oneself will become the measurement others use to value them. Someone who consistently devalues him/herself will ultimately not be taken seriously by others and vice versa.

People who are able to influence others are generally confident in themselves. They think and act positively. They believe they can fly and not fall. As a result, others believe in them and are willing to give them the chance to prove themselves. Generally, people like to be led by others who are stronger than themselves.

- **Communicate clearly**- People who are able to influence others can articulate their thoughts in the form of words, very clearly and succinctly. Their effective communication skills help them to relate at the same level as those they are trying to influence. They refrain from using complex words to impress others, focussing instead on developing a rapport with others. Their communication style helps them to relate well with others and eventually gain their trust.

- **Flexible-** There is tremendous power that comes with the art of flexibility. People, who can change their style to suit the environment they are in, are able to influence others best. We operate in a society where people have different values and cultures, which are sentimental to them.

19

People feel respected when others do not trash their values and beliefs.

Moreover, they feel honoured when others make an effort to adapt to their cultures as a form of respect. As a result, flexible people are more likely to be accepted and listened to, by others. Being flexible helps people to explore different perspectives of an issue before reaching any form of decision.

- **Good listeners-** As this aspect of relationship is so vital, we will be devoting a section to this subject later. For now, it is useful to note that the ability to listen to others effectively is a rare skill.

Effective influencers are acutely aware of this and consistently hear others well and engage in a two-way dialogue with them. Although, they know what they want, they do not allow their own personal agenda to stop them from listening to other people's point of view.

- **Integrity-** People, who are perceived as honest, are more likely to be able to influence others than those who are not. Integrity is about being seen to do what one is committed to. It is about being consistent in every sphere of life.
- **Persevering-** Effective influencers acknowledge that there will be challenges ahead. They prepare for these challenges but do not see them as obstacles to stop them achieving their goals. They press on towards their beliefs and goals irrespective of challenges. For them, when faced with problems or set backs, they use these as opportunities to learn and grow. They do not run at the first sight of trouble. Because of this, they strengthen their

knowledge and ultimately use it as a springboard to support their confidence.

When people perceive others as more knowledgeable than them, they are far more likely to be influenced positively by them.

- **Empathy**- Effective influencers are able to view things from different perspectives. Because they are able to step in other people's shoes to see things from other people's perspectives, they are generally perceived as reasonable, fair and approachable. People who are perceived as fair and understanding, are more likely to influence others.

There are other noticeable qualities of effective influencers, which we will simply summarise as:

- Sharing
- Good networks
- Professional
- Logical and factual
- Assertive

We will be expanding on some of these areas later. Taking all these points together, to increase your influencing power through your personality you need to:

- Be a person of integrity.
- Develop good listening skills.
- Be flexible in your dealings with others. Try to understand their concerns and find ways to achieve a win –win result.
- Value other people and treat them with respect.
- Communicate clearly, using appropriate methods to fit the situation you are trying to influence.

21

- Persevere in situations of crisis, knowing fully well that with time, the appropriate method to influence the situation will be discovered.

Expertise

People possessing expert knowledge are able to influence others in matters relating to their area of speciality. Most importantly, in organisations, others look up to leaders with expert knowledge to provide direction and guidance in pursuit of corporate goals and objectives. They are able to gain the trust of others, through their expert knowledge and can get others to do what they want. It is for this reason that people seek professional advisers to guide them through their decisions. People who want advice on electrical issues will seek advise directly from a professional and reputable electrician. Furthermore, a financial adviser will gain the trust of his/her clients in matters relating to financial planning and management. However the situation will be much different if he/she attempts to give advice in matters relating to building construction or plumbing.

As a manager, if your team perceives you as a true expert, they will be much more receptive when you try to exercise influencing tactics such as rational persuasion and inspirational appeal. And if your team sees you as an expert, you will find it much easier to guide them in such a way as to create high motivation.

If your team members respect your expertise, they'll know that you can show them how to work effectively. If your team members trust your judgment, they'll trust you to guide their good efforts and hard work in such a way that you'll make the most of their hard work. If they can see your expertise, team members are more likely to believe that you have the wisdom to direct their efforts towards a goal that is genuinely worthwhile.

22

Taken together, if your team sees you as an expert, you will find it much easier to motivate them to perform at their best.

To develop your expert power, you must:

- Develop expert knowledge in a particular area through formal training and education and/or practical experience.
- Ensure that people are made aware of your expert knowledge, using appropriate media. For instance, you can ensure that details of your qualifications and accomplishments are displayed in areas where people can gain sight of them easily. Your certificates from your formal qualifications can be displayed on your office wall; details of them can be included in your website and business card etc. Your accomplishments can also be included in office brochures.
- Ensure that you conduct yourself in ways that are consistent with your expertise. You must keep updating your knowledge so that it does not diminish with time. You must consistently portray and protect your expert image.

Information or network

Influencing through this source involves having access to or control over information or contacts, which others need but do not have.

It is well known that information is power. However effective organisations will continually strive for greater information sharing across the board, to mitigate the risk of concentration of information in the hands of few people.

23

People who are extroverts are usually disposed to high level of socialisation, which gives them a higher capacity to develop good networks and solicit invaluable information.

Furthermore, some jobs provide individuals with formal authority and control over certain types of information. If such information is useful to another party, their control of it could become a source of power.   In order to enhance one's networking power, a deliberate effort must be made to develop healthy relationships with others – this is what is referred to as networking skills. This involves taking active decisions and steps to meet others in formal and informal gatherings, and developing professional and healthy relationships with them. Some people do not value the power of network and more often than not disadvantage themselves by doing so. Here are some of the benefits of networking.

Networking provides opportunities to:
- Meet other people from different works of life
- Access information directly from people we know and through people we know
- Disseminate information widely to people we know as well as their own network. For instance, imagine someone who knows twenty people and want to advertise a business through them and to them. Imagine that each person (amongst the twenty) knows another twenty people. Just by knowing twenty people, you can immediately gain access to their contacts.
- Make useful relationships.
- Improve oneself through learning from others
- Understand the behaviours and personalities of different people.

24

A word of caution; whilst networking is important, spending too much time   networking can create an imbalance in ones work life.

The trick is to strike the right balance between the importance of strengthening one's information power and spending quality time in other areas that are equally important for effective results.

Position and status

As it says, this type of power is derived from the position or status of individuals in their jobs or any other sphere of life. Some positions in society, whether in an organisation or in a political arena, can provide a source of power. This is because they provide individuals with formal authority and power, to control resources and make decisions on how best resources are to be utilised. So for instance, a top official that controls budgets totalling over £100 billion can wield a significant position of power. A chief executive officer will generally have a higher authority and accountability than the receptionist. Consequently, others will accept the CEO as having some power over them because of his/her position. Similarly, managers with responsibility for resources (staff) will be perceived as having power over their staff by virtue of their position. Notice, that this type of power has nothing to do with knowledge or information that people have. It is merely related to their formal position in an organisation.

Consequently, the route to position power is taking steps to increase one's capability to hold senior positions in organisations or the society at large. Suppose you wish to become a Prime Minister in your country, which will result in increasing your position power, you must take steps to increase your interest and understanding of political matters with a view of becoming a member of parliament.

25

Similarly, if you require position power in a non-political world (e.g. in an office), you must take steps to increase your skills, knowledge and range of experiences that could provide you with the competencies required to hold senior positions.

You must be aware that although position and status power can be a source of influence on others, they must not be relied on exclusively when trying to influence people.

When we influence others to do what we want them to do, a number of outcomes can emerge:
- People willingly agree to what we want them to do and are genuinely committed to it.
- People accept that in principle what we are asking them to do sounds right, but they may have doubts about the feasibility of our proposal.
- People are indifferent to what we want them to do but go along with it (for a number of reasons- in the interest of social harmony etc)
- People accept our proposals grudgingly, because the other party has greater power over them.

When people are influenced primarily through position and status power, there is always the risk of them being resentful over time. The influencer wins and the other party loses. This is not a healthy position that any one should aim for, as more often than not, the decision taken will be short lived due to limited commitment by the other party. Successful influencing should be sustainable. It should aim for a genuine commitment from the other parties involved so that long-term relationships are not damaged.

Factors that can raise personal power
- Thinking positively about yourself
- High self esteem
- Managing stress
- Making choices
- Facing your fears
- Believing in yourself
- Dealing with negative feelings
- Commitment to yourself and life in general
- Being knowledgeable and well informed.

Factors that can decrease personal power
- Stress
- Illness
- Depression
- Tiredness
- Low self esteem
- Being frightened of risk
- Being negative
- Lack of confidence
- Not being sure of yourself or what you believe in or care about
- Ignorance.

Most people would like more power and influence. If you want to influence someone you need to:

- Build rapport and choose the best style to use for the situation
- Have the skills to put over your message (be assertive)

- Recognise your own and others' skills, personalities, sources of power and influence.
- Understand the culture, networks and relationships, which will have a bearing on your influence attempt.

Powerful people are secure and can give others power. Powerless people are often bossy and domineering, relying on their small power base because they are insecure.

Chapter 3

Influencing Model

So far, we have looked at what influencing is all about and the different sources of influencing power. We now know that developing our influencing skills creates tremendous benefits for us and the organisations we work for. We have explored the dynamics of human behaviours, with the view to understanding different personality traits to help us adopt different approaches when dealing with different people.

We will now turn our attention to different models of influencing, as well as influencing styles. We believe that these models should help you develop your capacity to influence others effectively, in the future, if they are learnt and used appropriately.

At this point, you already know that influencing is a skill that enables the achievement of results through other people. A person is effectively influenced, when he/she becomes genuinely committed to a course of action, which may be different to his/her original viewpoint. The emphasis is on genuinely committed.

Commitment is based on an individual's attitudes and values. Influencing relies on your understanding of a person's attitudes and values, establishing their existing commitment in a specific area and then using that information to gain a genuine commitment to action.

Let us now look at an example. Suppose we are trying to influence a client to shift from point D to point E. Perhaps we are trying to sell the client a new product or service or trying to get

29

the client to change their approach towards a particular situation. We will first show this in a diagram form, followed by an explanation.

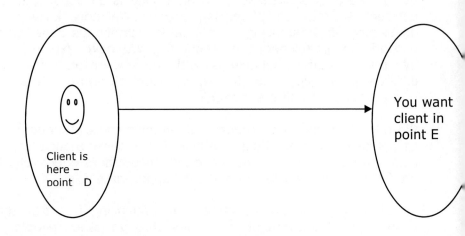

You first need to know where the client actually is. Understanding of this D point (i.e. an indication of a client's existing commitment) is a key aspect of influencing. Try to imagine that, if we all live at the top of our own hilltop this will be our point D.

Life teaches us to protect ourselves, our attitudes and value systems from outside attacks, by building strong defences. Because we have different attitudes and values, we have different viewpoints of our surrounding world. So, if a client is on their hilltop, in order to influence them, we must first climb to their hill top and get inside their castle (figuratively) in order to establish and understand their existing values, attitudes and commitments. This is not going to be easy.

30

Sometimes, we need to establish some common grounds first, then build enough rapport with them before we proceed.

Here are models that you can use to influence others.

Model 1

(PR) EDICT

This acronym covers both the process and the core skills needed to influence effectively.

PR	Prepare& Research	Find out what you can and set out your objectives
E	Entry	This phase of the process deals with building enough rapport and trust so that people will open their drawbridge to you
D	Diagnosis	A good look around the castle. A guided tour to attitudes, values and commitments. It is crucial at this stage that you learn to listen actively, without making assumptions and more importantly you must learn to suspend judgements.
I	Influence	After your guided visit, you will decide how best to influence-as you should now have all the necessary data.
C	Contracting	Having made your intervention you need to clarify and firm up on what will be done and by whom, with a view to achieving genuine commitment.
T	Transition	This is how we ensure that the contract is implemented. You need to maintain the relationship.

31

Preparation and research

Find out as much as you can about the person you want to influence.

Find out about what they are expecting:

- What their commitment is etc.
- What you want from them (i.e. your objective)
- What is or might be the person's viewpoint
- What common ground you have with them.

Entry

Entry issues are about rapport, competence and control. You need to create trust and confidence, reduce ambiguity and build on common ground. Flexibility is vital, as you may need to revise your plan as you go along. You will need to get agreement on common grounds.

Diagnosis

Your confirmation of perceived commitments and needs, tells you that you are on the right lines. You can ask questions like, what is the real issue and how important is the issue to you and why. The value and attitude data you get back, tells you if your proposals are likely to be received well or if you need to explore the issues further. Whatever else happens, the data you collect at this stage will point you to the right influencing strategy.

Influence or intervention

Think about, what your role is and what it needs to be; expert or catalyst.

Some influencing strategies you can use include:
- Make strong and definite proposals.
- Give information and clarify issues.
- Get the other person/s to explore alternatives and make some proposals.
- Expand the other person's views on the issues.
- Point out negative outcomes- the consequences of not acting on them.
- Appeal to and use commitments gained during diagnosis
- Confront issues.
- Get clients to join you in some problem solving activities.
- Use the big stick (if you have one) to gain agreement.

Contracting

You need a clear understanding of what has been agreed, which demonstrates an appropriate level of genuine commitment. Get agreement and this will be your contract. Successful influencing is not a win-lose situation. It is about two parties achieving a genuine commitment to something both are happy with.

Transition

This covers the proposed implementation sequence:
- What is to be done and by whom
- When is it to be done
- How is it to be done
- How will progress be checked
- Contingency plans

A good transition is the key to the next entry with this person. Leave the relationship with the care and attention you used to create it.

33

Model 2

Another method you can use which is quite similar to the previous model is the five easy steps model.

Five easy steps to influence

- **Gain rapport**- Get to the same level as the person you are trying to influence. Get to know their beliefs and values and match their behavior patterns, whilst blending your personality and characteristics with theirs.

- **Ask questions**- Elicit the needs of the person/s as the case may be and probe to identify their motives, attitudes and feelings.

- **Listen actively-** Demonstrate you are listening and listen with all your senses (your eyes, ears, feelings, heart etc). Suspend all forms of judgments that could impair effective listening.

- **Stress pertinent benefits**- Summarise how specific benefits of your proposal will accurately reflect their needs.

- **Work towards a decision**- Ask questions which will force a decision (or rejection). Test interest through hypothetical questions. Make positive statements, which assume their acceptance.

Before we move on to look at other different influencing styles, let us quickly conclude this section by providing you with an equation for successful influencing capabilities.

Influencing Equation is simply the sum total of:

Skills + Desire + Power

Where skills =Trust, expertise, honesty, unbiased, good communication, active listening, questioning, probing, awareness of non-verbal communication, positive thinking.

Where desire = Motivation to make things happen (enthusiasm, energy and so forth)

Where power = Expert knowledge, information control, status and position, internal strengths, confidence and high self esteem and so forth.

Influencing styles

In brief, there are four major influencing styles:

- Reward and punishment
- Rational persuasion
- Participation and trust
- Common vision

These are split into two types: "Push and Pull".

The style that is used at any given time will affect commitments and determine whether you will achieve success in the short term or in the longer term.

Pushing will influence people but only in the short term.
Pulling people will be more effective in the longer term and will maintain the relationship for the future.
"**Reward and punishment**" and "**Rational persuasion**" are pushing styles. "**Participation and trust**" and "**Common Vision**" are pulling styles.

There are several aspects to each style. We will now look at each style in summary together with the indicators for each style.

Reward and punishment (Push style)

"Do this or else..." "You do this and then you can do ......"

This influencing style **concerns using** pressures and incentives to control others. Rewards might be offered for compliance and punishment or deprivation for non –compliance. The influencer may use their own power or could employ more indirect methods such as using their status, prestige and authority to gain influence.

There are three aspects of the reward and punishment style:

- **Evaluating (E):** involves praise or criticism, approval or disapproval and the moral judgement of right and wrong.
- **Prescribing goals and expectations (PGE):** this is letting others know exactly what is required and expected of them and setting clear standards on how their performance will be judged.

36

- **Incentives and pressures (I&P):** applying incentives and pressures **involves** offering rewards or punishments.

Rational Persuasion (Push Style)

"It will be good if you do this now" "I'll stand by now while you do it"

This style of influencing others is characterised by logic, facts, opinions and ideas to persuade others. The basis for agreement and approval is the soundness of the other person's reasoning.

There are two aspects of the rational persuasion style:

- **Proposing (P):** people who use proposing behaviour are usually highly verbal and articulate. They are forward with their ideas, proposals and suggestions and they are not afraid of the reaction of others to them. Often they ask questions in order to present their own position on matters. They are persistent and energetic in persuading others.
- **Reasoning for and against (RFA):** the other aspect of rational persuasion is reasoning for and against, where people enjoy the cut and thrust of verbal battles. They emphasise logical argument rather than emotional appeal, marshalling facts for their own case and against their opponents. They listen to others only to find weaknesses in their arguments. Even when they are defending an inferior position, they battle away with determination.

Participation and trust (Pull style)

"Let's see if we can do it this way" "If I do this, could you do that"

The use of participation and trust pulls others towards what is desired or required by involving them.
By actively listening to and involving others, an influencer increases his/her commitment to the task, and in return, follows-up. Supervision then becomes less critical.

There are three aspects of the participation and trust style:

- **Personal disclosure (PD**): people who use personal disclosure openly accept their limitations of knowledge, mistakes or weaknesses. By their example, others feel accepted and do not have to compete for attention and control. Personal disclosure builds trust and willingness to be influenced.
- **Recognising and involving others (RIO):** this involves drawing out and listening carefully to the contributions of others and building on and extending those ideas rather than countering with alternative proposals. It is being quick to give credit for ideas and suggestions of others, and being willing to delegate responsibilities. By skilfully recognising and involving others, the influencer ensures that they work to solve the problem and are committed to the result, rather than resisting influence or blocking a solution.

38

- **Testing and expressing understanding (TEU):** by rephrasing or playing back what others have said, the accuracy of communication is checked and the other people feel their ideas are valued. Communicating understanding and acceptance of others' ideas helps others to know they have been listened to and increases their willingness and the receptiveness to be influenced.

Common vision (Pull style)

"Won't it be special if ……" "I have a dream…."

This influencing style aims to identify a common vision of the future for a group, and to strengthen the group members' belief that, through their collective and individual efforts, the vision can become reality. The appeals are to the emotions and values of others, activating their personal commitment to private hopes and ideas and channelling that energy into working towards a common purpose.

There are two aspects of the common visions style:

- **Articulating exciting possibilities (AEP):** this is communicating enthusiasm about possible outcomes of seemingly routine, as well as, unusual projects or challenges. Using images, they kindle excitement within others and help them imagine a better future.
- **Generating shared identity (GSI):** an individual appeals to common values and hopes in others, and helps them feel the strength, which comes from a unified group. The emphasis is on what we can accomplish, if we all work together to achieve common goals and ideals.
-

39

Looking at the above, you will see that influencing styles can fall into any of these categories:

- Logical approach
- Autocratic
- Collaborative
- Emotional appeal
- Assertive behaviour
- Passive behaviour
- Salesman approach
- Bargaining and so forth

We will now summarise the reasons why people resist being influenced. These may be due to:

- Different points of views
- Different values, agendas and beliefs
- Destructive motives for personal gains
- Lack of trust
- Emotional baggages
- Lack of objectivity
- Personality clash
- Inappropriate or wrong timing by the influencer
- Past negative experiences.

Chapter 4

Listening, questioning, communication and assertive skills

We will now explore in some detail four of the skills required for successful influencing.

1. Listening skills

Throughout this manual, we have emphasised the importance of listening skills, as one of the key tools you will require to influence others effectively. The table below summarises the key indicators of a trained and untrained listener. Your aim is to maximise the former and minimise the later in the way you relate with others.

AN UNTRAINED LISTENER		TRAINED LISTENER	
1.	Tunes out from the other person at the beginning- prejudges without giving the person a chance	1.	Defers judgement- is more controlled- listens to the persons feelings and situation.
2.	Is quick to criticise grammar, appearance or speaking style. All attention is directed to style.	2.	Pays most attention to content-not just to appearance, form or other superficial issues.
3.	Spends the time preparing to talk instead of listening. This is obvious and is often sensed by the talker	3.	Listens completely first- tries to get every nuance of meaning. Tries to really understand.

41

AN UNTRAINED LISTENER		TRAINED LISTENER	
4.	Tends to listen mainly for facts- specific bits of information, possibly errors, to pounce on to prove the other person wrong.	4.	Is more mature in his/her listening habits. Listens for the main idea and disregards minor points.
5.	Tries to take in everything- tries to reply to everything especially exaggerations and errors	5.	Concentrates only on the main issues. Does not worry about replying to everything and avoids side tracking remarks.
6.	Fakes or pretends attention	6.	Gives himself internal cues to listen.
7.	Divides his attention or tries to do something else while listening.	7.	Does one thing at a time-as they know listening is a full time job.
8.	Gives up when they realise they have to work actively at understanding what the person is trying to say	8.	Listens carefully. Sorts, gives feedback and asks for confirmation.
9.	Tends to get distracted by emotional words- Does not control his emotions; sometimes loses his temper and responds inappropriately.	9.	Feels anger but controls it. Does not allow his emotional reactions to govern his behaviour.

2. Questioning skills

Asking the right question is the key to getting the right answers and will enable you to take control of conversations. You will need to get **a** lot of data to make a successful diagnosis and therefore increase the likelihood of a successful influence.

Types of questions

There are two main types of questions:

Open questions- are used when you want to get more information, or if you need to get shy or quiet people to talk a bit more. People have to talk when asked open questions.
This can be useful when you are dealing with people who are angry or upset. It enables them to express their feelings. Open questions begin with:

- What...
- Where...
- When...
- Who...
- How...

Closed questions- can help you to get to the point and ask for specific answers. A simple "yes" and "no" can answer them. They are useful when you are dealing with a person who is long-winded and vague. They are also helpful for getting and checking details. They begin with:

- Do...
- Did...
- Can...
- Is it...
- Are you...

43

Other types of questions

Probing - An open question that helps to pursue a line of thought in greater depth. Probing questions are usually specific.

Leading- Questions indicate the answers you would like/expect to hear. Leading questions can be useful as a last resort to prompt someone to reply.

Loaded - These types of questions imply a judgement or criticism. They can produce a defensive response. They can be implied by the tone of the voice as well as the words, e.g. "You cannot be serious...

Multiple- Several questions strung together. Respondent can choose which one to answer.

Limited alternatives- offer a choice of responses, e.g. "Is it because of "x" or "y".

Mirroring – Repeating the last few words of a reply, usually with a questioning intonation. Encourages further comment.

Linking – These are questions that refer back to something mentioned earlier and demonstrate that the speaker is being listened to. They ensure ideas are not lost but avoid interruption e.g. "you mentioned earlier that ………."

Prompting - Encourages continuity by nods, the words yes and no, sympathetic noises etc.

Effectiveness in questioning

It is generally believed that open and probing questions are the most effective in encouraging both the quantity and quality of a response. Leading, loaded and multiple questions may produce misleading responses and loaded questions can be very damaging to the climate of discussion.

Closed questions can be valuable in moderation, to establish facts but used to excess, they give the feel of an interrogation, with the questioner having to work very hard.

For the questioner, it is important to recognise your natural questioning style and to be aware of its effect on a discussion and the quality of information generated. It is important to develop skills in selecting the most appropriate form of question and related techniques, to achieve your chosen purpose.

3. Assertive skills

Assertive behaviour was cited earlier on as being one of the characteristics of successful influencers. As we have a separate manual that covers this subject in depth we recommend you use it to explore this subject in depth. For this reason we will only provide you with a brief point on this subject.

There are three simple basic steps to assertiveness. It is important that individuals learning to be assertive understand and practice all three and in the right order. At the start, there seems so much to take in and do but with practice it becomes almost second nature.

Step 1 – Actively listen to what is being said then show the other person that you both hear and understand them.

Step 2 – Say what you think or feel

Step 3 – Say what you want to happen.

Step one forces you to focus on the other person and not use the time they are talking to build up a defence or attack. By listening you are able to demonstrate some understanding and empathy for their situation or point of view even if you do not wholly agree with it.

Step two enables you to directly state your thoughts or feelings without insistence or apology.

Try to use good linking words between step one and two e.g. however, on the other hand, nonetheless, in addition, even so, alternatively etc. Try not to use unhelpful ones like "but" as it may sound like you are contradicting your first statement.

Step three is essential so that you can indicate in a clear and straightforward way what action or outcome you want without hesitancy or insistence.

Once the three basic steps to assertiveness have been learned, there are a number of key assertive behaviours and techniques which add to the competence and confidence of assertive people. You can find these techniques in our manual titled "**Strategies For Building Your Assertive skills**".

4. Communication skills

When we communicate with others we transmit messages through the words we use, our body language and our voice tone. It is well established that our body language plays a significant part in face-to-face communication regardless of the words we speak. Next is the tone of our voice, followed by our choice of words.

55% of what we say is communicated through our body.
38% of what we say is communicated through our voice (tonality).
7% of what we say is communicated through words.

Consequently, what we say must match our body language if we are to be assertive. A word of caution; interpreting body language can be a tricky business. This is because body language is affected by cultural factors, which can carry different meanings in different contexts. Therefore, we urge you to treat the next examples as relating mainly to the western culture. In some African cultures, minimum eye contact is seen as a sign of respect towards elders whereas too much eye contact is interpreted as a mark of disrespect.
Some cultures are tactile, whereas others are not. We can now review the different types of body language in relation to the three main types of behaviour.

Behaviour	Posture	Facial Expression	Eyes	Speech & Voice	Gesture
Assertive	Upright Relaxed Open	Committed Concern Interested Responsive	Eye contact	Direct Calm Gentle Friendly	Open Hands below elbow Parallel shoulder
Passive	Bent Crooked Slumped	Blank Uninterested Afraid	Looking down Minimum contact	Quiet Weak Hesitant Slow	Restless Nodding head in agreement Pinching flesh
Aggressive	Rigid Tight fist Clenched teeth	Tight jaw Glancing Frowning Eyes squinting	Staring Glazed over	Fast Loud High pitched Demanding Opinionated	Pointing Finger wagging

Final thoughts

Now that you have completed this manual, we recommend that you take steps to develop an action plan for areas you will need to focus on in your quest to develop your influencing skills. For some people, developing an action plan will involve soliciting honest feedback from others in respect of how well they fare in some of the personal skills required for successful influencing.

Whilst reading this manual will provide you with the knowledge required to further your personal development growth plan, like all training programmes, you will need to master the art of putting the knowledge into practice, yourself.
In short, personal development is only accomplished, when behaviours change to align with those that lead to success.

Finally, it is always advisable to keep your action plan at a manageable level to avoid being overstretched.

As a valued customer, we request that you contact us with your feedback (and suggestions) on any aspect of our training manuals you believe needs further improvement or clarification. We value your feedback, as part of our commitment to provide you with the best "Self Study Training and Development Programme" that will help you maximise your potential in business management.

Further readings from BSS learning series which are available from our website below are:

Financial Management
Introduction To Financial Management
How To Evaluate Business Financial Performance
Strategies For Maximising Cash Flow
Budgeting For Success

People Management
Introduction To Management For New Managers
Strategies For Building Successful Teams
Managing Staff Recruitment, Selection and Induction
Managing Staff Performance Effectively

Interpersonal Skills
Strategies For Building Your Assertive Skills
Strategies For Communicating Difficult Messages At Meetings
Time Management Strategies For Busy Managers

Future developments

Over the next twelve months, we plan to develop more training manuals that will provide you with further technical knowledge and skills required in general business management. We urge that you continue visiting our website to keep abreast with our latest products development.

Our website details:

www.businessservicessupport.com

About The Author

Sheila Elliott is a Professional Accountant and a Fellow of the Chartered Association of Certified Accountants (ACCA). She holds a Bachelors of Science degree with honours in Economics, as well as a Masters in Business Administration (MBA).

Sheila has over 17 years experience in senior and middle management role working for major national and international voluntary and public sector organizations. She currently holds various directorship positions with well known voluntary sector organizations and has helped numerous businesses improve their business management systems, staff development and financial management systems. She is renowned for her professionalism, thoroughness, insights and ability to achieve successful results using innovative and creative approaches.